CCSS **Genre** Fantasy

M000110867

Essential Question
What buildings do you know?
What are they made of?

Staying Afloat

by Vita Jiménez
illustrated by Gaia Bordicchia

This is Sam. This is Sam's boat. The boat is his house.

Sam likes to live on a boat.
He likes to float here
and there.

The wind blows. Sam likes to go fast on his boat. Down the river he floats!

Sam sees Bob.

"Hi, Bob," says Sam.
"What is that?"

"It will be a boat," says
Bob. "Can you help me?"

5

"Yes," says Sam. "This will be fun."

Bob and Sam make the boat.

"Will it float?" asks Sam.

"Yes, it will," says Bob. "Let's go!"

"Jump in when I say
go," Bob says. "One, two,
three, go!"

Sam jumps in. Bob jumps
in. Then the waves
jump in!

Bob's boat is going down!
Bob falls out, but Sam
can help.

"Thank you, Sam," says Bob.
"You are a good pal."

"Could you help me again?" says Bob.

"With what?" Sam asks.

"Can we make a new boat?" says Bob.

"Yes," says Sam. "Let's try again!"

Respond to Reading

Retell

Use your own words to retell events in *Staying Afloat.*

Character	Setting	Events

Text Evidence

1. Who are the characters?

   Character, Setting, Events

2. What does Sam do after Bob falls out? Character, Setting, Events

3. How do you know this story is a fantasy? Genre

CCSS **Genre** Nonfiction

Compare Texts
What can you do on a houseboat?

A Day on a Houseboat

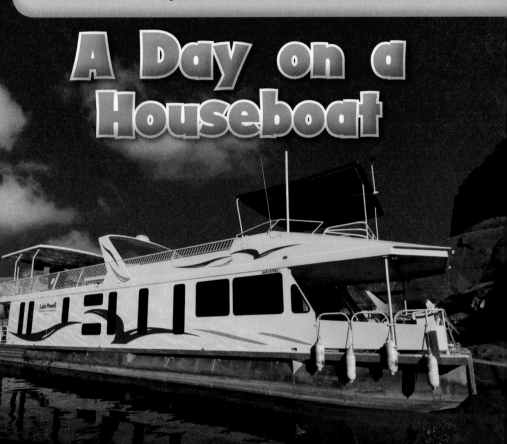

Is this a house? Yes.
Is this a boat? Yes.
It's a houseboat!

What can you do on a houseboat? You can fish. You can cook food and eat it, too. You can even sleep in a bed!

A houseboat deck is a nice place to sit with friends.

A houseboat kitchen looks just like a kitchen in a house.

This bedroom is in a houseboat.

Make Connections

How is living on a houseboat like living in a house? Text to Text

Focus on
Genre

Fantasy Fantasy is a story that has made-up characters, settings, and events.

What to Look for In *Staying Afloat,* the mice talk, wear clothes, and build things. Mice don't really do these things.

Your Turn

Make up a story about an animal that builds things. What does the animal build? Write down your ideas. Draw a picture to go with each idea.